Mindset, Model, Money

Mindset, Model, Money

52 Amazing Tips to Help You Build a 6-Figure Business

Kimberly Chenier, Esq.

authorHOUSE

AuthorHouse™
1663 Liberty Drive
Bloomington, IN 47403
www.authorhouse.com
Phone: 1 (800) 839-8640

© 2015 Kimberly Chenier, Esq. All rights reserved.

No part of this book may be reproduced, stored in a retrieval system, or transmitted by any means without the written permission of the author.

Published by AuthorHouse 08/26/2015

ISBN: 978-1-5049-3349-0 (sc)
ISBN: 978-1-5049-3348-3 (e)

Library of Congress Control Number: 2015913783

Print information available on the last page.

Any people depicted in stock imagery provided by Thinkstock are models, and such images are being used for illustrative purposes only.
Certain stock imagery © Thinkstock.

This book is printed on acid-free paper.

Because of the dynamic nature of the Internet, any web addresses or links contained in this book may have changed since publication and may no longer be valid. The views expressed in this work are solely those of the author and do not necessarily reflect the views of the publisher, and the publisher hereby disclaims any responsibility for them.

Contents

Part One - MINDSET 1

TIP #1	Begin with the End in Mind	3
TIP #2	Know Your WHY	5
TIP #3	Have a Mission Statement	8
TIP #4	Know the Value of Your Business	11
TIP #5	Set Goals	14
TIP #6	Set BIGGER Goals	16
TIP #7	Reorganize Your Thoughts	18
TIP #8	Reframe Your Thoughts	20
TIP #9	Release the Negative	22
TIP #10	Retrain Your Brain to a Better Belief	25
TIP #11	Repetition, Repetition, Repetition	27
TIP #12	Your Belief Changes Your Reality	29
TIP #13	Success Should Always Be the Expected Conclusion	32
TIP #14	Have a Vision	34
TIP #15	Create a Vision Board	37
TIP #16	Create a Vision Statement	40
TIP #17	Have a Mindset of Giving	43
TIP #18	Do What You Love	46
TIP #19	Delegate	48
TIP #20	Be in Community with Like-Minded People	51
TIP #21	Have a Role Model	54
TIP #22	Hire a Mentor, Coach, or Consultant	56

Part Two - MODEL 59

TIP #23 Clearly Communicate the Benefit of
Your Product or Service 61

TIP #24 Do What You Love (Part 2) and Do It Well 64

TIP #25 Be a Lifelong Student 66

TIP #26 Be the Expert 68

TIP #27 Give Yourself an Expert Title 71

TIP #28 Have a Niche 73

TIP #29 Have a System 76

TIP #30 Know Your Ideal Client 79

TIP #31 Fill the Gap 83

TIP #32 Have a Marketing Message 85

TIP #33 How to Deliver Your Product or Service 88

Part Three - MONEY 91

TIP #34 Have a Leveraged Business Model 93

TIP #35 Use Multiple Streams of Income 96

TIP #36 Have Active Income Streams 98

TIP #37 Have Passive Income Streams 100

TIP #38 Price Your Products and Services for
Maximum Cash Flow 102

TIP #39 State the Price, Then Shut Up 104

TIP #40 Always Have an Upsell 106

TIP #41 Take Action 109

TIP #42 Implement, Implement, Implement 112

TIP #43 Stop Procrastinating 114

TIP #44 Make a Decision 116

TIP #45 Work Smarter, Not Harder 118

TIP #46 Use Your Blogs to Make Money 121

| TIP #47 | Use Podcasts to Make Money | 123 |
| TIP #48 | Networking That Pays Off | 125 |

BONUS TIPS 129

TIP #49	Renew Your Enthusiasm Every Day	131
TIP #50	Pace Yourself	133
TIP #51	Stay Focused	135
TIP #52	Take Care of Yourself	137

Introduction

Statistics claim 80% of all new businesses will fail. The word "fail" is harsh because a majority of businesses don't actually fail; the reality is that business owners simply quit! Why? Because owning and operating a business isn't easy, and if you don't have the right tools and training, for some, quitting becomes the better option.

Being an entrepreneur is both exciting and scary. For those who come from a family of entrepreneurs, learning how to run a successful business was probably taught to you in childhood. For first-generation entrepreneurs, it's trial and error. Whatever your starting point, entrepreneurship can be learned.

I've discovered success leaves clues. If you follow those clues, you too can be successful! A few years ago, I started studying successful entrepreneurs. I read lots of books and attended lots of business seminars and trainings. I carried a little notebook with me wherever I went. Whenever I read or heard a nugget of successful business advice, I would write it down in my notebook. When that notebook was about half full, I read through it and saw a pattern that connected all those nuggets. I knew I had uncovered a goldmine of information.

This book is a combination of my research and almost two decades of hands-on experience as an attorney.

How to Use This Book: This book is designed to give you one full year of business building tips, one week at a time. You can choose to learn and practice each tip for one week, or you can read the entire book and learn at your own pace. No matter how you choose to learn, the key is if you practice all the tips in this book, you'll have everything you need to build your 6-figure business.

Part One

MINDSET

The most important part of building a business is starting with the right mindset.

If you talk to any successful entrepreneur, they will tell you a big portion of their success is directly related to their mindset. Yes, you must have confidence and a double dose of fearlessness. But more importantly, you must know without a doubt, what you want, why you want it, and how you will go about getting it. And, you must be of the mindset that if you do not achieve the intended goal, you have not failed and you will not quit. You will learn what you did wrong, set another goal, and keep moving forward.

Success does not come easy; you have to work hard for it. Some of the hardest work you will do on the road to building your 6-figure business is staying in the right frame of mind to handle the pressure of being an entrepreneur.

TIP #1

Begin with the End in Mind

Beginning to build your business with the end in mind means you have already thought about your end goal and what it will take you to get there, the end goal being a profitable business that consistently generates 6-figures or more each year. If you're not clear on what you want, how will you know when you get it?

Knowing where you want to end helps you formulate the plan and put together all the necessary pieces to achieve your goal. In order to hit 6-figures, you need a business model that is designed to make money. Most businesses fail due to lack of planning, not knowing your market, and not having a system for making money.

When you begin with the end in mind, your focus is sharper, your decisions come quicker, your marketing is more effective, and you waste less time because you're not doing anything haphazardly. You have a goal and a concrete plan to reach that goal.

What is your end goal? Before your start building your business, devise the step-by-step plan to get you there.

NOTES:

TIP #2

Know Your WHY

Why do you do what you do? Most people would say, "To make money." Making money is the end result of what you do. But think about it again. Why do you do what you do? What is your purpose for getting up each day and working in your business?

When you are clear on your WHY, you get excited and passionate about it. And when you are excited and passionate about what you do and why you do it, potential clients notice that and they want to do business with you.

Here's a little secret about building a successful business—and this is probably completely opposite of what you currently think or have been told. But I promise, if you embrace it, the sky's the limit for you and your business.

Ok, here it is: make your business about more than just making money!

Tony Hsieh, the CEO of Zappos summed it up well when he said,

"Chase the vision, not the money; the money will end up following you."

If you know your product or service provides a solution to people's problems and you get excited just thinking about how you're going make their lives better, then that's your WHY.

Your WHY is your connection to potential clients. They are drawn to you through your WHY. Your business will stand out in the sea of sameness because of your WHY. And when you stand out, you get more business. As Tony Hsieh says, "The money will follow you."

If you want to learn more about how to inspire people with your WHY, read *Start With Why* by Simon Sinek.

What is your WHY?

NOTES:

TIP #3

Have a Mission Statement

Successful entrepreneurs know where they are going and put in place a mission statement to help them focus on getting there. A mission statement, which is sometimes also called a purpose statement, is a powerful tool that provides you with a path for success.

You can create a personal mission statement or a company mission statement or both. Many successful entrepreneurs including Oprah Winfrey, Virgin Group Founder Sir. Richard Branson, and founder of "The Daily Worth" Amanda Steinberg have mission statements. You can bet some of the world's largest corporations such as Coca Cola, McDonalds, and Google have mission statements cast in stone.

Your mission statement should include these three elements: the value you create in the world, who you are creating it for, and the outcome you expect. For example, Oprah's mission statement is "To be a teacher and to be known for inspiring my students to be more than they thought they could be." Oprah may not have been a classroom teacher, but she became one of the world's best-known inspirational teachers of humanity.

Drink in this example of a corporate mission statement from Coca Cola: "To refresh the world, to Inspire moments of optimism and happiness, to create value, and to make a difference." If you operate your business according to your mission statement, you won't get sidetracked or veer away from the plan you designed for success.

Using the three elements above, create your mission statement. Then read that statement every day until it is engrained in your brain. Your mission statement will become the essence of how you show up in the world.

NOTES:

TIP #4

Know the Value of Your Business

By "value" I'm not talking about the monetary valuation of your business, but rather, is there value in your product or service? That means, is there a market for what you are selling? Are there customers willing to buy what you are selling?

For example, when gas prices are high, the demand for large gas guzzling vehicles declines and there is very little if any value in selling those types of vehicles. Or, when there is a drought, the demand for umbrellas is zero! Be clear on what you offer and confirm there is a large group of potential clients who need what you are offering.

Do your research before you start your business. You must see what the marketability of your product or service is and what you can do that is different from other businesses in your same niche. Conduct surveys through an on-line survey company, hire a survey specialist, or you can do the market research yourself by asking friends, family, co-workers, neighbors or anyone else who would be a potential client.

Often, not only will you find out if there is a market for your product or service, you will also get clues about exactly what your potential clients need and how to make your product or service better meet their needs.

If you find out there is no market for your product or service, no value in it, then don't give up, just make adjustments. Come up with alterations to your original idea or create another idea completely on how you can share your gifts with the world.

Is there value in you business?

NOTES:

TIP #5

<u>Set Goals</u>

Continuously set goals throughout the life of your business. There will always be higher levels of success to which you want to or need to aspire.

You should have short-term and long-term goals. Sometimes goals can be overwhelming, but if you break them down into mini-goals or milestones within the larger goal, they are always achievable. If your goal is to offer a new product or an additional service, first research all you can about the idea, and then learn everything you need to do to make it happen.

Make a list of all your goals, starting with the end goal (see Tip #1). Then fill in the short term goals and milestones you need to accomplish on your journey to the end goal.

NOTES:

TIP #6

Set BIGGER Goals

In addition to your average goals, set a few BIG goals too. Make the goal so BIG it scares you! When you do this, your brain may say, "You can't do that" or, "What makes you think you're going make that happen?" Fear, anxiety, non-belief, and doubt may set in. If that happens, tell yourself, "Yes, this scares me, but I want to achieve it and I will achieve it."

Go forward, face your fear, and do it anyway (see Tip #9). Ask for as much help and guidance as you need from those who already achieved that same goal. You can do it, I know you can!

NOTES:

TIP #7

Reorganize Your Thoughts

Any thought, feeling or behavior that moves you away from your goals cannot be allowed to dwell in your mind. You cannot give life to the negative chatter in your head that says you can't do something.

Most of the time negative chatter is a result of something that began way back in your childhood. The crazy thing is, it's not even real—at least not anymore! It's time to stop allowing negative thoughts access to the forefront of your thinking.

The negative chatter and stories you tell yourself disempower you and keep you stuck. Your life is a reflection of the stories you tell yourself. You can make the choice to stop re-living the story from your past so that you don't keep living it in your future. You make the choice, your story or your destiny, you can't have both.

Identify the negative chatter that has been holding you back and start working on putting that in your past.

NOTES:

TIP #8

Reframe Your Thoughts

When negative chatter pops up, reframe those thoughts to positive thoughts, feelings, or behaviors. Dismantle the negative. Think positive. An example of this concept of reframing is, if you saw a big chunk of iron sitting on a table, don't just see it as a chunk iron. See the possibilities within that chunk. Somewhere in there is a screwdriver, screws, bolts, watch springs, and an endless number of other useful items that can be forged from that chunk of iron.

Reframing lets you take a chunk of useless nothings and cast them into a whole host of useful somethings. Regard the negative chatter in your mind as useless babble that doesn't fit with who you really are and what you're capable of achieving.

What would your life look like if you reframed your negative chatter?

NOTES:

TIP #9

Release the Negative

As you reframe your thoughts, start to release the negativity, fear, doubt, and anything else that moves you away from achieving your goals. This is not an overnight process, but if you are committed to it, you will start seeing results immediately, possibly in days. You may never be totally rid of the fear, but that's ok. Just learn to feel the fear, accept it, move through it, and don't let it hold you back.

Some fear is real and some fear is imaginary. A real fear is suddenly seeing a lion who has just escaped its cage and is racing towards you with its mouth open. An imaginary fear is thinking you will die if you give a speech in public. Fear is a mechanism your body uses to protect you and keep you safe. Fear stops you in your tracks and makes you retreat. That is good when you come face to face with a hungry lion, but when building a business, fear can be your biggest obstacle.

What I have learned is you can change the way you process fear. The next time you feel fear rising up inside you, do these steps: First, identify the source of the fear, is it real or is it imaginary; next, if the fear is imaginary, reframe the way you see the fear (see Tip #8); then, take action in the face of fear. That's right, look that fear straight in the eye and take action! If you practice this each time you feel fear, you will begin to have amazing breakthroughs, including a boost to your confidence. And before you know it, you will have released those negative feelings associated with your fear.

NOTES:

TIP #10

Retrain Your Brain to a Better Belief

After you reorganize your thoughts, reframe your thoughts, and release the negative thoughts, then it's time to retrain your brain to adopt a better belief. You can do this with positive affirmations about yourself and your business.

As with releasing the negative, retraining does not happen overnight, and it's something you will have to work on daily. Go to your local bookstore's self-help section and purchase affirmation cards, research them online, or better yet, write them yourself.

You will know which thoughts need to be retrained, so start writing those affirmations on post-it notes. Stick them up in every room of your home, and on the dash of your car. Read them aloud every day until they become second nature and you can just recall them on command.

Be intentional. Motivate yourself. Be your own biggest cheerleader!

NOTES:

TIP #11

Repetition, Repetition, Repetition

Repetition is the foundation of learning. Repeat a good habit every day and watch it become a part of your belief system.

Use this week to repeat positive affirmations to yourself.

NOTES:

TIP #12

<u>Your Belief Changes Your Reality</u>

When you replace a negative thought with a strong positive belief, your reality has changed significantly and for the better. Now you have high-powered ammunition that will give you a much better chance at achieving your goals.

A new positive reality that is in line with your business and personal goals puts you in harmony not only with achieving those goals, but also with building business success beyond belief.

There was a story on the Oprah Winfrey Network about a man named Nick Vujicic. Nick lives in Australia. He surfs, snorkels, golfs and plays soccer. Nick married the love of his life. Sounds like a typical guy, right? Nick Vujicic was born with no arms and no legs.

Sometimes he uses a wheelchair to get around, but most of the time he doesn't and it's amazing to see him maneuver his body and play sports the way he does. Nick told Oprah he was harassed and tormented in school and he even attempted suicide at the age of 10.

Nick said it wasn't until he discovered the power to take control of his life that his life changed for the better. When Oprah asked Nick what made him chose to take control of his life, Nick answered "it's all about choice, you can be angry for what you don't have or you can be grateful for what you do have."

Choose to change what you believe about yourself. Choose to change your reality.

NOTES:

TIP #13

Success Should Always Be the Expected Conclusion

No matter what the goal, always expect you will be successful in achieving it. Expect nothing less than success in whatever you do!

As you go through this week, expect everything you do will have a positive outcome. Don't let your mind drift to a negative result. Tell yourself how a situation will work out. Speak it out loud. Set the expectation and watch how things work themselves out.

NOTES:

TIP #14

Have a Vision

A vision is necessary to help you focus on where you want your life or business to be next year, five years, or ten years from now. Where you or your business is now is just your starting point.

Your vision should be clear. What exactly do you want to achieve and what steps are necessary to get there? Many people create vision boards (see Tip #15) to help them keep their vision in focus until it miraculously becomes their new reality.

If you have no vision at all, you will be stuck in the same place forever. If you have a vision but it is small, you will never know to what extent you could have made a change in the world.

Think about some goals you have for yourself right now. Are they small, or have you taken those goals and visualized them to their highest level?

You have to remember that everyone will not see your vision, and that's ok. The great sculptor Michelangelo started with what everyone but him saw as an unfinished block of marble. But when he looked at that marble he envisioned the amazing Statue of David. Michelangelo saw what was possible when others didn't. Henry David Thoreau said "It's not what you look at, it's what you see."

What goals and visions for your life do you have that you know can be expanded? Stop dreaming small and start creating your life of endless possibilities.

NOTES:

TIP #15

Create a Vision Board

Many successful people have created a vision board. This is their vision statement (see Tip #16) in pictures. It can encompass your personal or business goals.

Your board could contain an image of a book to represent your vision of publishing your own best-seller. Your board could contain an image of a microphone on a stage in front of hundreds of people, which represents your vision of being on stage in front of large crowds. Your board could contain an image of a beautiful building, which represents your new storefront that you will open as an off-shoot of your booming online store.

Whatever the vision, find images that represent it, and make it your own. Most people put their vision board in a place where they will see it every day, maybe in your office, or bedroom, or bathroom. After a while, those images become seared into your memory. Your brain doesn't see these as dreams, it thinks of them as real, what you're supposed to have. Your subconscious mind does not differentiate between wishes and reality, so your visions are your reality!

Start gathering images of what you want your future to be. Take those images and create your own vision board. Look at it every day, and see your vision become your reality.

NOTES:

TIP #16

Create a Vision Statement

A vision statement is different from a mission statement. As discussed in Tip # 3, your mission statement contains the value you wish to create in the world, who you are creating it for, and the outcome you expect.

Your vision statement is the end result of achieving your goals and putting in the hard work. For example, it may be elation for having sold one-million products or gratitude that your services transformed one-million lives. Your vision statement could also include those things you will reward yourself with: a big new house or brand new car you'll be able to now afford with your business earnings. Your vision statement speaks to the end result or proceeds of all of your goals.

In essence, your vision statement is your vision board put into words. For example, if your vision board contains photos of people smiling which represent your satisfied customers, and it also contains photos of a beautifully furnished home, part of your vision statement could say "I am grateful that my product or service has helped so many people and that has allowed me to buy the home of my dreams."

When you look at your vision board daily, and recite your vision statement daily with gratitude, it will be just a matter of time before what you envisioned for your business and your life, becomes your reality.

NOTES:

TIP #17

Have a Mindset of Giving

Make no mistake, entrepreneurs are in business to make money. But why not consider structuring your business to not only make a profit but also do good in the world. The purpose of receiving is to enjoy, but also to enjoy giving to others. It's the natural order of the give and take of life. See what life your business and your happiness take on when you keep this balance.

You will attract more customers if you have a mindset of giving. People are more likely to do business with you if they know not every dollar they spend with you goes directly into your pocket, but that some goes to help charities, philanthropic ventures, and individuals or groups who simply need help.

In the Zappos shoes business model successful business owners are truly fulfilled not just from what they earn but also from what they give. Giving opens you up for more having. You can give of your time, talent, or money, and you will have more joy, peace, happiness and abundance! It's giving that breed's success, not the other way around. That's a secret not many business people have come to realize.

Kimberly Chenier, Esq.

If you don't already do it, try giving to those who need help. This is how you truly become rich. Not rich with money, but rich in character and rich in spirit.

NOTES:

TIP #18

Do What You Love

One of the richest entrepreneurs in the world, Malcolm Forbes, once said, "Success follows doing what you want to do. The biggest mistake people make in life is not trying to make a living at doing what they most enjoy."

Why not do what you love? It is that thing that you most enjoy doing that comes easiest to you and gives you the most joy. How can some profit also not come from that? You've probably heard people who love their jobs or professions say that what they do doesn't feel like work. That's because they love what they do.

The most common trait of genuinely happy people is they paid attention to and followed the longings in their heart. In other words, they are doing what they love. Spiritual Entrepreneur, Teacher, and Philanthropist John Assaraf says, "Do more of what you love, less of what you tolerate, and none of what you hate." That makes perfect sense not only when applied to living one's life in general, but also in the business world. Work at what you love and you'll never work a day in your life!

NOTES:

TIP #19

<u>Delegate</u>

You cannot do everything, even if you think you can! Please don't think less of yourself by getting help. It doesn't make you any less of an entrepreneur. You have a special gift or talent, and that gift needs to be focused on the larger picture of how to build the business.

Help is all around you, even if you don't see it. If you're starting out small, hire a virtual assistant (VA) to do only the tasks you designate. A virtual assistant is just that — virtual. You communicate via phone, email, Skype or use other handy communications technology that are constantly springing up. Your VA can do any job that doesn't require them being in the same room with you.

Hire a VA to work a couple hours a week or full time, whatever your needs happen to be. They can perform work by contract on a one-time or intermittent basis. VA's are everywhere these days, fulfilling roles in many professions and trades. It's becoming a more popular, smarter way to work, and a great resource, especially for startup businesses or sole proprietors just starting out. Remember, only do what you do well, and let someone else do the rest.

Make a list of the things you do best, then delegate the rest!

NOTES:

TIP #20

Be in Community with Like-Minded People

As you build a business, it's critical to have the support of someone who understands your journey. You may need to bounce an idea off someone or ask for guidance on how to do something. Maybe you could benefit from a business mentor, or someone who you can shadow for a few days.

Make sure you have a support group of people that you respect, have numerous contacts and resources that align with your business, and are willing to give you their time.

It's not that difficult to find other entrepreneurs at various stages of the business cycle. Benefit from the expertise of those who are working on getting there, are almost there, and have made it to where you want to be.

Search on-line groups such as "Meet Up" where you can find entrepreneurs just like you, in your same area of business. There are endless numbers of networking groups such as LinkedIn, Rotary Club, and specialized groups that match your business type or goals.

An especially helpful place to meet contacts and potential business partners is at seminars, conferences and live events which focus on your areas of business. Always attend with plenty of business cards, an open ear, and a willingness to get involved in the group's activities. Then passing along your business card and making connections gets more traction. Remember, you're making friendships, and exchanging advice. It goes both ways.

NOTES:

TIP #21

Have a Role Model

Whatever your area of business, there are always one or a few people at the top of their game who have "made it." Find someone who has your same values and business goals and pattern your business after theirs. I'm not saying copy someone else; you should always be original. What I am saying is in "patterning" your business after their's, you have a ready-made model of their success. You're not starting from scratch.

Find out what steps they took to get where they are, their pitfalls and how they bounced back from them. If they've written a book, read it. If they give lectures or speeches, attend them.

If you can arrange to meet them and speak for a few minutes it will be time well spent. Learn whatever you can from those who have traveled the path ahead of you. One day, when your business is a big success, you will be someone else's role model.

NOTES:

TIP #22

Hire a Mentor, Coach, or Consultant

If you're not sure how to build your business—and believe me, most of us had that issue at the beginning stages—then hire someone to help you. Some people refrain from hiring this type of expert, as they feel their money might better be spent using it for more immediate or tangible aspects of the business. However, the money that goes towards hiring someone who can help you reach your goals is the most important "investment" in your business.

When you plan your business budget, you should include a line item for business growth. Most experts have invested a lot of time and money in themselves to get where they are. Why not take advantage of that knowledge and experience to help you grow your business?

There is a saying that goes, "Let my long road be your short cut." In other words, why not shorten your learning curve by letting an expert show you how quickly you can make a business grow?

If you'd like to work with me in building your 6-figure business, please go to **www.builda6figurebusiness.com**

and email me through the "contact us" page. I would love to be your guide and help you develop the mindset to create the model that will generate 6-figures and more in your business!

NOTES:

Part Two

MODEL

Your business model is the secret sauce to the entire business. Without it, you are just hoping you make money. You need a plan to make the money and a model to do it.

The Harvard Business Review defines a business model as consisting of "interlocking elements that, taken together create and deliver value." Most importantly, it's to create value.

The most successful companies are those that have figured out how to create a solution to a fundamental customer problem.

Your model consists of what you offer, who you offer it to, and how you offer it. From your model, you will create a signature system, which is what you will use over and over again in various forms and mediums to generate income.

TIP #23

<u>Clearly Communicate the Benefit of Your Product or Service</u>

Be very clear on the product or service you provide. In order to effortlessly attract customers, you must communicate how your product or service benefits them within the first seven seconds of talking to a potential client.

Potential clients don't care what you do, they care about how what you do will benefit them. Ever heard of WIIFM? That stands for "what's in it for me," and that's all the potential client wants to hear from you. Your business model should always focus on the benefit to your customer.

Example: If you sell back scratchers, what you are really selling is a way to satisfy that annoying itch that your arm can't reach! See the benefit for the customer, satisfy that annoying itch, and that's exactly what your marketing should say.

Another example: If you are a nutritionist, what you are really selling is a healthy long life free of daily medication. That's what people want. They don't want a diet or exercise program, but they do want a healthy long life! Think about your product or service, then extract the benefit that solves someone's problem. That's what will attract customers.

What is the benefit you provide?

NOTES:

TIP #24

Do What You Love (Part 2) and Do It Well

As already discussed in Tip #18, if you build your business doing something you love, success is practically guaranteed. Now take that a step further and do what you love better than anybody else. Matter of fact, do it so well that you create your own niche.

Maya Angelou said it best, "You can only become truly accomplished at something you love. Don't make money your goal. Instead, pursue the things you love doing, and then do them so well that people can't take their eyes off you."

Separate yourself from the pack and stand out by doing what you love, and doing it better than anybody else!

NOTES:

TIP #25

Be a Lifelong Student

You are the foundation of your business. Without you, there is no business. You can eventually structure your business to run on systems which you can turn over to someone else, but while you are building your 6- or 7- figure business, YOU are the foundation.

Whether you're selling a product or a service, our world is constantly changing and so should your business. Learn everything you need to know about it before you open your doors, and keep learning as the business is growing.

Technology changes rapidly; ways of communicating change rapidly. You must keep up with the latest trends and changes and adapt them into your business. If you're stubborn or afraid of change, if you don't continually expand your knowledge and learn and accept new business practices, trends, and advancements, you and your business will be left behind.

Sometimes, learning a new skill is as easy as going to Google and watching a tutorial. Other times it will mean you have to hire a coach, or attend classes. Whatever you do, make the commitment to yourself and your business to keep learning and keep growing.

NOTES:

TIP #26

Be the Expert

You won't be surprised to know that whatever your business, there are probably hundreds or even thousands of others running that same type of business. So, in order to be seen and heard, you must stand out in your field. The best way to do that is by positioning yourself as the expert!

As an expert, you become the authority in your field, and authorities get more attention. People pay top dollar for expert advice and expert solutions.

I heard a story once that goes like this:

The hub for FedEx is located in Memphis. It's a huge building and every FedEx package has to go through the Memphis warehouse before reaching its final destination, so this warehouse needs to be running 24/7.

One day, everything in the warehouse comes to a halt. Conveyor belts stop and all the lights go off. The power shuts completely down. Every minute the warehouse is not operating costs FedEx thousands of dollars, so they need to get the power back on quickly.

A repairman is called, he looks around, and cannot find the source of the power outage. A second repairman is called, he takes a look and he too cannot find anything. A third repairman is called. He looks around, walks over to the control panel, pulls out his screw driver and turns a screw. Voila – everything comes back to life, and the warehouse is up and running again.

The warehouse manager is very appreciative and asks the repairman how much is owed to him. The repairman says "$10,000." Well you can imagine the look on the manager's face. He tells him it only took 15 seconds to turn that screw. "Why do you think we should pay you $10,000?" The repairman asked for a pencil and paper. He writes something down and hands it to the manager. The manager looks at the paper, shakes his head in agreement, walks to the safe, pulls out $10,000 in cash and pays the repairman.

Now, I bet you're wondering what was written on that paper. Here's what it said: screw driver $1.00, knowing what screw to turn and how much to turn it $9,999!

Get the point? Being the expert means people pay you what you are worth.

So how do you become an expert? You learn everything you need to know about your business and its products or services. Then you tell people you are the expert by assigning yourself an expert title (see Tip #27).

What can you do better than anyone else? Find your expertise and let everyone know you are an expert.

NOTES:

TIP #27

Give Yourself an Expert Title

It's easy for a person who teaches you how to do something or gives you advice to call themselves an instructor, coach, or consultant. But that doesn't exactly separate you from the pack.

Example: A person who helps you maintain a healthy diet is usually a nutritionist or dietician. Sometimes they may call themselves a health coach or health counselor. Those titles are a dime a dozen. Your probable response: So what? You can find dozens of them everywhere, on Google, Craig's list, or through other on-line searches. And, since there are so many folks with that same title, they all start to run together you just end up choosing the one that is closest to your area.

But what if you called yourself "The Queen of Healthy Eating" or "Healthy Lifestyle Expert." Are those not interesting titles that grab and impress you? Not only do people want to know more about you when your title is out of the ordinary, they also believe you have more expertise, more status, and are the "go-to" person in that field.

Now it's your turn to give yourself an expert title.

NOTES:

TIP #28

Have a Niche

A niche is a distinct segment of a market, area or field. If you want to build your business quickly, then focusing on a specific niche market is your answer.

Once you become the expert (see Tip #26) and give yourself an expert title (see Tip #27) you're able to carve out a very specific segment of a larger market and design your business to satisfy the needs of that niche market.

Example: Our Healthy Lifestyle Expert (see Tip #27) may teach people how to create healthy meals, but that's a little broad. Chances are there are probably many experts in this field.

What if our expert narrows down that market into healthy meals for busy moms? That's a great niche! Can you make that niche even narrower? Yes! Healthy meals for busy moms in 30 minutes or less! Now, our healthy lifestyle expert is an expert in 30-minute healthy meals for busy moms.

You see how specifics can work? There's going to be a large market for that service, I guarantee. That business niche has solved three problems: 1) healthy meals; 2) for busy moms (probably without a lot of complicated ingredients); and 3) prepared in 30 minutes or less. You could take it a step further by creating shopping lists and weekly menus too (see Tip #40). It's genius!

What is your niche?

NOTES:

TIP #29

Have a System

Service providers such as coaches, consultants, instructors, teachers, or anyone who advises others on how to do something, should always have a "system" they use with each client. Your system should be unique and tailored especially to the service you provide.

Generally, our brains can only remember three separate pieces of information at a time. So, many service providers have a "three-step system." However, "five-step" and "seven-step" systems work very well too. And, always make the system an odd number because, well ...that's just the way our brains work.

Naming your system is important, but not just any name. Your system must be something that describes WIIFM (see Tip #23). If there's nothing in it for the customer, you lose.

Example: If your system is called "Seven Steps to Seven Figures" you are going to attract everyone who wants to learn how to make seven figures. And, since it's created by you, using your unique proven content, then you can claim it as your proprietary system. All of your marketing and selling points should be centered around your unique branded system, that of teaching people how to make seven figures.

Start thinking about what you do over and over for each client. Or, what questions do you answer repeatedly for your clients. That can be a start to creating your very own system.

NOTES:

TIP #30

<u>Know Your Ideal Client</u>

Who is your client? Who needs what you are offering? Who will spend money on your product, program or service? If you can't answer those questions in detail, then your business will never go to the 6- or 7-figure level.

Why do you need to be clear on exactly who your ideal client is? Because you should only be marketing your business to the people who need it. There's a saying, "If you try to sell to everyone, you will end up selling to no one."

All successful businesses know exactly who their ideal clients are, and that's who they market to. McDonalds knows who their customer is for each of their menu items. Toyota knows who is interested in each of their car models. Starbucks knows who drinks their mocha lattes, and Macy's knows who shops in their intimate apparel department.

You too, must know who wants your program, product or service. But how do you figure it out? Some if it is common sense. For example, our Healthy Lifestyle Expert (see Tip #27) knows first and foremost, his/

her customer is someone who wants to eat healthy meals, or someone who may be overweight or has a preventable disease such as high blood pressure or diabetes, which can be controlled through diet, exercise, and a healthy lifestyle. But to dig deeper, is the ideal client male or female, married or single, kids or no kids? What income level?

There are quite a few variables that go into identifying your ideal client. But I promise you, once you have narrowed it down, identified the demographics of your customer, found a price point they are willing to pay, you can then kick back and focus on marketing to that ideal client. Because when you've found them, you've found a lot more customers saying "yes."

So what's the best way to create an ideal client profile? Do a brain dump of every aspect of the ideal person for your product, program or service. Write it all down and then give your ideal client a name. You've just isolated your ideal client and can stop wasting time with those who have no interest in spending their money with you.

Our healthy lifestyle expert has no use for athletes, body builders, fitness gurus, or anyone else who is already living a healthy lifestyle; that's a waste of time.

So next, how do you find your ideal client and what they want? The best way is to ask them! Know your ideal client, then go where they go. Go to association meetings, meet-ups, parties, gatherings ... anywhere your ideal clients hangs out. Talk to them, even ask if they will fill out a short survey (for this you should offer them something in return). People will tell you what they want, so listen and learn.

NOTES:

TIP #31

Fill the Gap

Your potential clients are always in need of something. Look at it this way, where they are now is their starting point, and their end point is where they want to be. Between where they are now and where they want to be is the "gap" that your product, program or service must fill.

In my case, my clients either are not sure how to build a business, or have tried to build one and are not having a lot of success. All my clients want to have a successful 6-figure business. My services are the gap. I teach entrepreneurs a system for generating consistent cash flow, which allows them to build a 6-figure business. See how that works? My services fill the gap. Your program, product or service should fill the gap and be the solution to your ideal client's problem.

What product, program or service do you provide? How does it fill the gap for your ideal client?

NOTES:

TIP #32

Have a Marketing Message

You may have heard of an "elevator pitch," a statement about what you do that should take no more time to explain than a ride in an elevator. A marketing message is sort of like an elevator pitch, except it is tailored directly to your ideal client.

The difference between a marketing message and an elevator pitch is that an elevator pitch talks about what you do, and a marketing message talks about the transformation your ideal client will receive. See the difference? One is about you and the other is about your ideal client.

You want to always be talking benefits to your ideal client, what they need, and what you can do for them. No one wants to hear about what you do! Remember: WIIFM (see Tip #23). To develop a strong marketing message, you first need to know what your ideal client is asking for, what specifically do they need (see Tip #30).

Your marketing message should be phrased in your ideal client's language. When you ask them what they want, use their words to create your message. Let's use our Healthy Lifestyle Expert (see Tip # 27) as an example: Moms may be saying, "I need more time." Since no one can add a 25th hour to each day, what mom is really saying is, "How can I get everything done in the time I have?" The answer to that question is the Healthy Lifestyle Expert's solution and the transformation he/she provides. That becomes the marketing message, and it should include something about time. Here's how the Healthy Lifestyle Expert's marketing message should read:

> I help busy moms who don't have a lot of time between their kids' activities, and are stressed out about what to cook, prepare delicious healthy meals every day in 30 minutes or less!

This marketing message addresses the issue moms have about not having enough time, and how to get a healthy meal prepared for the family in the time she does have. See how that works?

What is your ideal client telling you they need? How can you turn that into a marketing message?

NOTES:

TIP #33

How to Deliver Your Product or Service

Your business model method of delivery will depend on whether it is a product or a service you are delivering.

For a product, selling options include sales through a retail store, an on-line store or website, an e-commerce retailer such as Amazon, a catalog, a vendor or participant at an event such as a farmer's market, and other non-traditional outlets. I always suggest selling products in all of the above ways. Don't limit yourself on product selling opportunities. Every business needs multiple streams of income (see Tip #35).

For a service-based business, you also have many options. You can work with clients one-on-one or in groups, in person or virtual, at retreats, or through books, video, and home study. Whatever delivery model you choose must, as with producers of products, include multiple streams of income (see Tip# 35).

What is your method(s) of delivery?

NOTES:

Part Three
MONEY

The key to generating consistent cash flow in your business is to make sure your business model is leveraged, meaning you must make sure there are several different ways to make money with your product or service. Keep in mind, the key to a successful business model is multiple streams of income. You design the model. You determine how much money you will make.

A leveraged business model is your path to significant wealth.

TIP #34

<u>Have a Leveraged Business Model</u>

McDonalds used to be known for its hamburgers, but have you looked at their menu lately? They sell salads, chicken wraps, rib sandwiches, fish sandwiches, kid's meals, ice cream, etc. That is a leveraged business model, with multiple streams of income. Everybody doesn't want a hamburger, but maybe they like the fries, so they'll buy a fish sandwich with their fries, or a chicken wrap with fries.

McDonalds and every other successful business figured out that if you can offer multiple items with multiple price points all based around your expertise, you ultimately generate a larger profit.

A product could be created in different sizes and with different features, all at different price points. You no longer sell only one item, you sell multiple items which appeal to multiple buyers.

For a service-based business, your offerings can be vast. For example, if you are a coach or a consultant, and you offer a program called "Five steps to Happiness," you can offer the entire course, and, you can offer each step as a mini-course. The information stays the same, you don't have to re-create anything, so you are not using any more manpower. But you have leveraged your main course into six different offerings.

How will you leverage your business to generate the most amount of income?

NOTES:

TIP #35

Use Multiple Streams of Income

After you design the plan to leverage your business, the next thing is to create multiple streams of income.

In the coaching and consulting industry, multiple streams of income include coaching programs, books, e-books, recorded audios and videos, home study programs, speaking engagements, and workshops. Under the banner of coaching programs, you can have one-on-one and groups which can be live or virtual, VIP programs, membership programs, luxury retreats, and the list goes on.

And the good thing is you can price each of your offerings at a different price point, so there is something that is affordable for everyone.

I've been told every business should have at least seven different income streams.

What income streams can you create for your business?

NOTES:

TIP #36

Have Active Income Streams

Active income requires you to do something to earn the money. For example, the money you make from a live training or one-on-one coaching is active income because you had to be there to actively participate.

Your time is valuable, so your highest source of revenue should be your active income. This is the part of your business where you up your fees.

Speaking engagements are also active income, but when you speak, you should always be marketing your business and selling your products.

Speaking may not generate a high paycheck, but it will pay off in the long run because it's the one way you can get many of your ideal clients in one room at the same time and close many sales from one talk. That's leverage and an income stream rolled into one!

When you become the expert at the top of your field, you will probably have fewer active income streams, but the ones you have will be at higher price points. Remember, your time is valuable.

NOTES:

TIP #37

Have Passive Income Streams

Passive income is the money you make while you sleep!

Unlike active income, you only have to do something once to derive passive income. You write a book once, then you get paid royalties every time someone buys it. You record a course on audio or video and get paid every time someone buys that home study program. And, your recorded audio or video home study course can now generate multiple passive streams with a mini-course (see Tip #34).

Your passive streams of income must contain content that has value. If someone is going to pay for a home study course, it must have proven benefits that someone is willing to learn without being in a live setting. But rest assured, there are lots of coaches and consultants out there who are making 6-figures and more using passive income as part of their business model, so it can be done.

What are your passive streams income?

NOTES:

TIP #38

Price Your Products and Services for Maximum Cash Flow

Pricing is totally up to you. If what you offer is unique and no one else is doing what you're doing, you can charge more money... and you will get it.

But beware. Setting the wrong price can kill your business. Setting your prices too low could make people wonder why you come so cheap. Setting your prices too high could price you right out of your market. You will need to do some research to find out what your competitors are charging, then price your offerings accordingly.

Your prices should be consistent with your field or industry, unless you have something that is unique or you are at the top of your game. Then by all means, charge more! My advice is to always charge what your product or service is worth.

NOTES:

TIP #39

State the Price, Then Shut Up

You should never state the price of your product or service until you have had a chance to tell the potential client about all the benefits it provides, and how their life will be much better after they say "yes."

Once you have done that, state the price and shut up. That's right, stop talking. Most people say the price, then try to justify it. If you have done Tips #23, #31, and #32 correctly, there is no need to justify the price. You've already done that through communicating the benefits the client will receive. All you have to do is say the price and wait for their "yes."

Of course you will get your "let me think about its" and "I don't knows" and you can reiterate the benefits to them. What you should never do is reduce your fee in order to get someone to say yes. That makes it look like you are in the business of negotiating for your product or service. What you can do instead is offer a payment plan that works for the client. Just be sure you design the payment plan to receive all payments before the final services are rendered.

NOTES:

TIP #40

Always Have an Upsell

Once you have a satisfied client, you want to keep them as a customer for life. How do you do that? You offer them additional products or services that also solve a problem or meet their needs. If you are a service provider (coach, consultant, teacher, instructor, etc.) and the service you offer solves a problem for your client, once that problem is solved your client will most likely develop a new problem which needs to be solved. This is called Problem/Solution, Problem/Solution, and should be part of your business model.

Example: Our Healthy Lifestyle Expert (see Tip #27) solved the problem of busy moms not having enough time to prepare meals for their families by teaching them how to create healthy meals in 30 minutes or less. Now your client has a new problem: what to prepare each day.

The Healthy Lifestyle Expert can upsell the mom into her next coaching package consisting of weekly menus and "done-for-you" grocery shopping lists. Again, this service upsell fills the gap (see Tip #31) for the busy mom and solves the additional problem.

You should aim to create the right upsell that seamlessly flows the customer from one offering to another. And, the price point for each upsell should be more than the prior offering. When you get good at this, you will be able to generate massive amounts of income.

NOTES:

TIP #41

Take Action

Every tip in this book means nothing if you don't take action. Successful entrepreneurs got that way by making decisions and taking action. In order to build a 6-figure business you must be a decision maker and an action taker.

Taking action doesn't always mean you will make the right decisions. But that's ok, because if you are in motion, if you are moving towards the goal, any misstep you make can be corrected.

Have you ever heard of course-correction? You may veer off a little, but you correct yourself and get back on track. Many, many business owners have failed more than once before they got it right and became a success.

You may know the story of Thomas Edison. The story goes, he failed 1,000 times before he got it right. But, had he not continued to take action and stopped with failure number 999, we would all be in the dark! Not really. Someone else would have come along after him and created the light bulb. But my point is, don't give up, learn from missteps, and take action to keep going.

If you are having trouble taking action due to fear, go back and read Tip #9

NOTES:

TIP #42

Implement, Implement, Implement

You've created awesome products or programs, you have a plan to provide excellent service, you have a vast knowledge in the area of your expertise. Now it's time to implement. John Assaraf once said, "Knowledge is not power, but the application of knowledge is power." That is so very true.

You can have an advanced degree or have taken specialized courses to gain a wealth of knowledge, but if you don't do anything with that knowledge it's not powerful, it's powerless. Your business will not grow, your client base will not grow, and your bank account will not grow if you do not implement.

Get out there, start implementing, and start building your 6-figure business now.

NOTES:

TIP #43

Stop Procrastinating

You were born to do great things. Every day you wake up is another opportunity to leave your mark on the world. Procrastination stops your forward progress. Procrastination is caused by fear. Re-read Tips 8-12 and make today the day you break free of fear, doubt, and limiting beliefs. You have everything you need to take the next step in building your 6-figure business. Don't put it off until tomorrow, start today.

NOTES:

TIP #44

Make a Decision

In the book *The Power of Decision* Charles Barker said it best, "Indecision is actually an individual's decision to fail." Whatever decisions you make in your business, make it, and be committed to it.

The problem arises when you are "wishy-washy" and "sit on the fence" pondering what you should do, or when you wait to see what everyone else is doing before you decide what your next step is. Don't do that! Be decisive with a clear "yes" or "no." The quicker you are able to make decisions, the quicker you will get to 6-figures.

NOTES:

TIP #45

Work Smarter, Not Harder

There are a number of ways you can automate your business to attract clients and make money without you being there. One way is through your website. Your website should be automated to offer visitors something free in exchange for their name and email address.

If you don't have an opt-in offer on the home page of your website, you are missing out on being able to communicate and sell to every potential new client that visits your website.

Additionally, if you don't need a full website, you can set up a landing page, which is generally there to get potential clients to opt-in for a free webinar, teleseminar, e-book or other gift of value in exchange for their name and email address. This is how you build your list of potential clients, the ones to whom you will market new offers.

How would you like to attract 10, 20, 30 or more new potential clients a day just by having a free opt-in offer? I think you would love that, so make sure you have that set up on either your website or landing page.

Your website is also the vehicle by which you make passive income. Clients purchase your home study courses, your books, your audios or videos through your website. If you don't have an automated sales system such as Constant Contact or Infusionsoft, then you may be missing out on a lot of money!

NOTES:

TIP #46

Use Your Blogs to Make Money

Blogging is one of the best ways to get attention in your field. If you blog on a regular basis, people will begin to notice you. You can even get paid as a guest blogger or contributor for a larger blog site.

The key to blogging is to pack your posts with valuable information, so readers will want to hear more and more from you. Now here's the juicy part. Once you have enough content-rich blogs, you can turn them into a book or a series of e-books that you self-publish and sell. You become a published author, which adds more credibility to your expertise, you've created a passive income stream, and you can use the book as a marketing tool for your business.

NOTES:

TIP #47

Use Podcasts to Make Money

If you'd rather talk then write, you can create your own podcast. Podcasts are your very own audio show which you use to market your business. You can have guests or you can fly solo and talk to your listeners on different topics or have different themes for each show.

You can monetize your podcast a few ways. One way is to allow people to listen to a portion of the audio for free and if they want to hear more, they have to pay.

The most common way to monetize your podcast is through advertising and sponsors. Sponsors use a formula to determine how much your audience is engaged with your podcast and how likely they are to purchase the advertised product. If you're good at what you do and you have an eager following you can attract sponsors to your podcasts and use that revenue as an additional income stream (see Tip #35).

NOTES:

TIP #48

__Networking That Pays Off__

Most of the time we think of networking as gathering with a group of people, business cards in hand, and going around the room telling people what you do and asking if they need your services. But, if you want your networking to lead to money in your bank account, you have to change the way you network.

In Tip #23 you learned to clearly communicate the benefit of your product or service, and in Tip #32 you learned that you must have a marketing message. When you have a marketing message that clearly communicates the benefit you provide, potential customers will flock to you. No longer will you have to nervously stand around handing out business cards hoping someone will call you.

Your clear, benefit-packed marketing message acts like a magnet for anyone who needs the services you have to offer. Instead of you asking, "Would you like my card," you will get people asking, "Tell me more about what you do" and "Can I get one of your cards?"

Make sure your card has your marketing message on it, so people will remember you, and that it has your website or landing page address clearly printed so people can opt-in for your free offer and get on your list of potential clients.

Networking can be fun, if you know how to do it right.

NOTES:

BONUS TIPS

TIP #49

Renew Your Enthusiasm Every Day

Building a 6-figure business takes time, patience and hard work. It can get frustrating and there will be days when you want to give up. But, if you did the work and created your Mission Statement (see Tip #3) and your Vision Statement (see Tip #16) then you can renew your enthusiasm for your business each and every day.

You should start your morning reading both your Mission Statement and your Vision Statement. But don't just read them, feel the emotion you first felt when you wrote them. Let your mind reflect back to your excitement when you first embarked on this journey of building a 6-figure business. Do this every day and before you know it, you will be reaping the rewards of your hard work.

NOTES:

TIP #50

Pace Yourself

Simply put, don't try to do everything all at once. Set your big goals, then set the mini-goals and milestones that you will achieve along the way (see Tip# 5 and #6). If you get tired, take time off. Building your 6-figure business is a marathon, not a sprint. Pace your strides along the way and you will make a strong finish!

NOTES:

TIP #51

Stay Focused

While you are building your 6-figure business, you are going to be tempted to do something else. Never fails, just when you get deep into building your business model, someone will give you a piece of advice on how you should do it differently.

Don't get sidetracked! Thank them for their advice and keep your eyes on your prize. You are the boss, you make the decisions, you know what's best for your business. Don't let someone or something else take your focus off your end goal.

NOTES:

TIP #52

Take Care of Yourself

Make time for you! When you feel the frustration coming on, stop, take a deep breath, and do something for yourself. Even if it's as simple as taking a hot bath by candlelight, make sure you take care of yourself.

Don't beat yourself up or feel guilty if you really need to get away from the business for a little self-care. Remember, you are the business, and you must always make sure you are physically and emotionally in a place where you are able to run it. I want you to remember and reflect on a translation of a popular line from the Toni Morrison novel *Beloved*: "You are your own best thing."

Treat yourself special, love yourself, and take care of yourself. Now go build your 6-Figure Business!

NOTES:

www.ingramcontent.com/pod-product-compliance
Lightning Source LLC
Chambersburg PA
CBHW030753180526
45163CB00003B/1012